A timeless journey of inspiration
and beauty through the eyes of a brave
and kind saint whose legacy empowers us
to be a force of good in the world.

Dedicated to
the people of
Ukraine
and to our
Swedish ancestors
from Småland

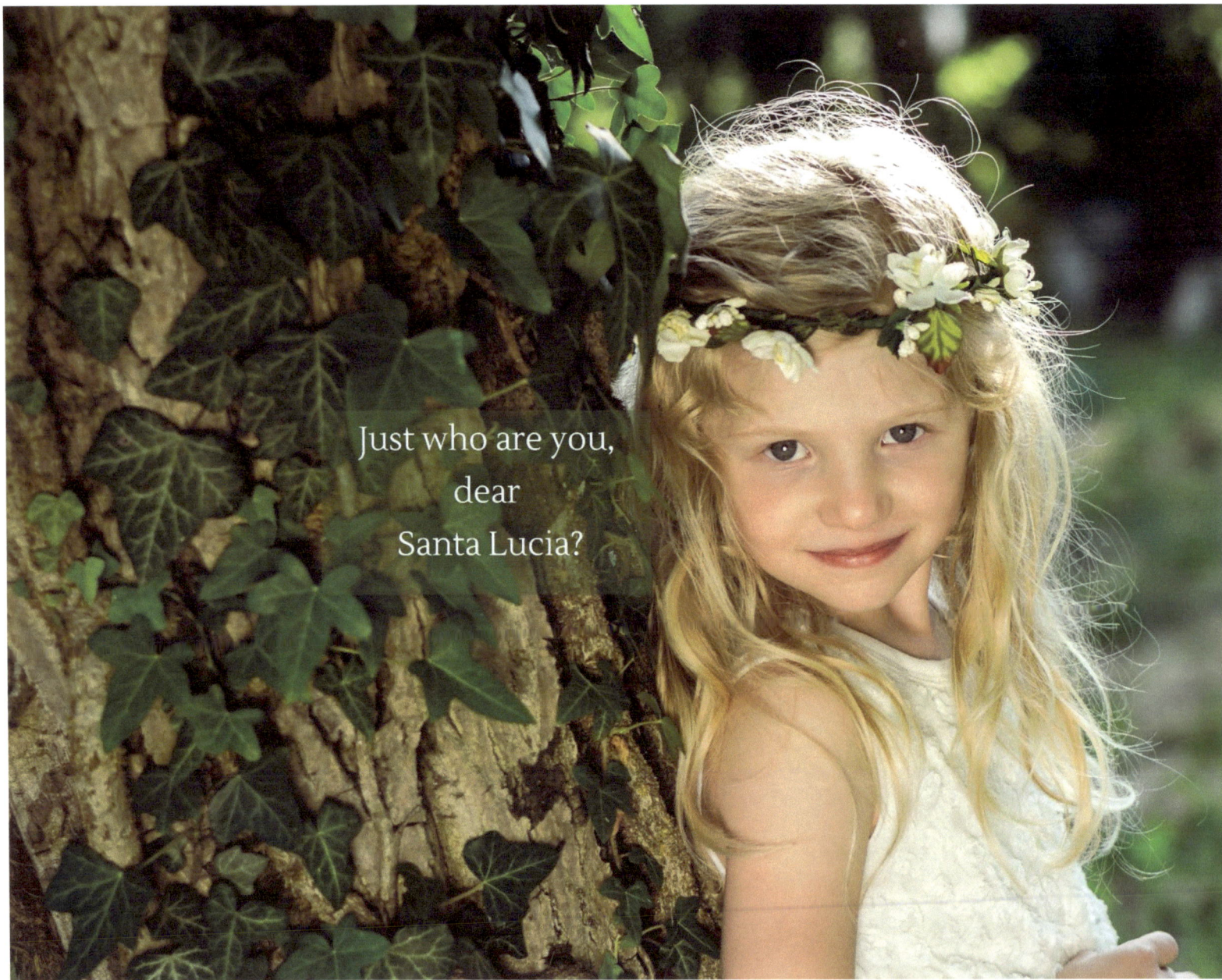

Just who are you,
dear
Santa Lucia?

I see you
standing there

wearing a white dress
with a red sash
and a crown of candles
on your head.

You look beautiful and magical,
with all those candles
glowing above you!

and I wonder...
who are you?

I, Santa Lucia
have come to
remind you
that even
when it is dark,
there is still light
and hope.

I am here to remind you that during those dark,
difficult times when you may feel lost, hurt, sad,
afraid, mad or lonely, there is still light
and hope and love
You are not alone!

When I was on
earth so many years
ago in the country
of Sicily,
I had everything
I could want. I also saw
many people in need
and suffering.

So my purpose
in life became a
wish to bring
hope and light
to others.

I chose to
bring food
to the hungry
and care for
the poor.
I chose to be
kind and brave.

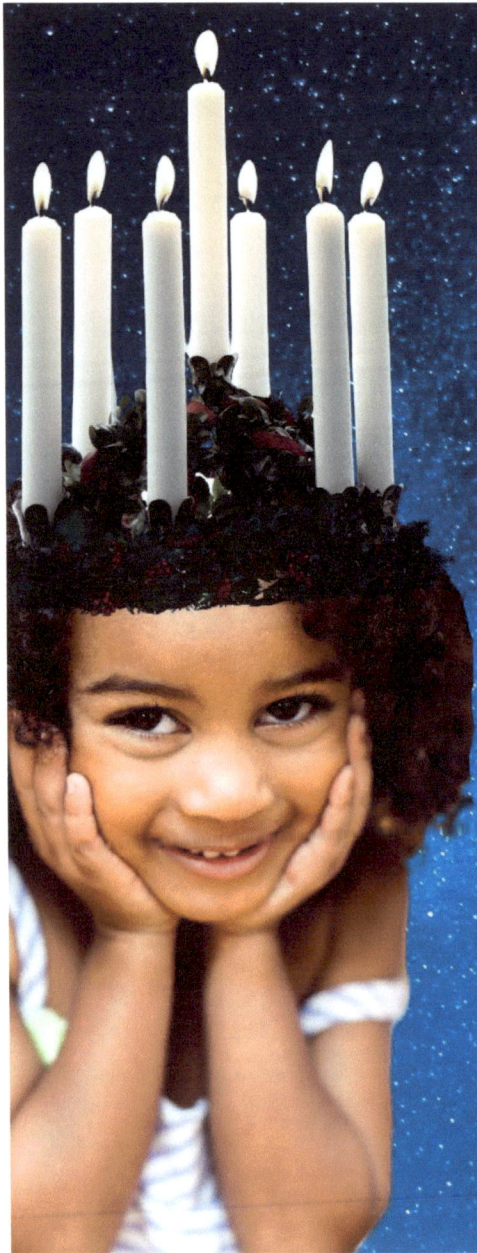

The story of my kindness traveled to
other countries, including Sweden,
where I am celebrated every year on
December 13th,
one of the darkest days of the year.

It is especially nice to celebrate the light
in Sweden because during Swedish
winters, there is not much sunshine!

Can you imagine the daytime being dark
most of the winter?

That is one of the reasons
why people in Sweden
love to light their
Lucia candles...
to brighten those cold winter days.

Do you know someone
who lives in Sweden?

Santa Lucia Day is also celebrated in many other countries including: Croatia, Denmark, Estonia, Finland, Hungary, Italy, Malta, Norway, Sicily (where I lived!) Spain, St. Lucia in the Caribbean, United States, and Venezuela.

I want to share with you,
one of the songs
written about me.
It is translated from
Swedish into English.
This song is often sung
as part of the
Lucia Queen tradition.

Santa Lucia Song

Night walks with a heavy step
round yard and house
as the sun sets over the earth.
Shadows are brooding.

There in our dark house,
Walking with lit candles,
Santa Lucia, Santa Lucia!
Night walks grand, yet silent,
Now hear its gentle wings,
In every room so hushed,
Whispering like wings.

Look,!
At our threshold stands,
White-clad with light in her hair,
Santa Lucia Santa Lucia!
Light your white candles,
Santa Lucia Santa Lucia!

And now that you
know about me,

you also might choose to
celebrate Santa Lucia Day
by imagining that
you are wearing
a white dress,
with a red sash
around your waist
and a crown of candles
on your head.

You might decide to
get up early one morning
and bring a tray of rolls and cookies
to someone special.

It's kind of like bringing them breakfast in bed!

Can you just imagine
smelling those rolls and coffee?

All throughout the year, there are so many
ways that you can bring this love and light
to yourself and to the world.
You can be kind and brave with your family,
friends, classmates, teachers and
people you do not yet know.

Here are some of the countless ways to help bring light into our world:

1. Bring food to the local food pantry.
2. Raise funds for a charity.
3. Visit or call someone who is ill or hurting.
4. Stand up for people who are being bullied.
5. Make friends with those who don't feel included.
6. Volunteer at a soup kitchen.
7. Recycle and reuse.
8. Keep filling yourself up with love and light!

I know how good
it feels to be kind and brave
and I believe that you have
the power to help make
this world a better place,
each time you bring light and
hope to yourself and others!

May this story of Santa Lucia give you courage

to bring your love and light to the world.

The world needs your kindness and bravery.

The world needs you to be a force for good.

"Even in a world that is being shipwrecked,

remain brave and strong."

~Saint Hildegard of Bingen

As we come now to the end of this book,
I want to share a blessing with you that
comes from the Book of Common Prayer:

Go forth into the
world in peace

Be of good courage

Hold onto that which is good

Support the weak

Help those who are sick

May it be so!

Appendix

Because meditation can help us stay
connected with the love and light that
is inside us, I offer this practice to you!

If you would like to hear me guide you
through this meditation, you can listen
on the audiobook version.

A Guided Meditation:
Connecting with Love and Light

If you would like to experience this meditation,

I invite you to close your eyes,
and imagine that you're in a most
beautiful favorite place.

Here in this special place, you can
notice all the colors and shapes that
surround you.

Take some time now to sense
into the sounds and smells.

Imagine that the sun is
shining over
your whole body.

You can feel it's warmth
and it is safe and comforting.

Breathe in deeply as you feel this warm golden light moving from
the top of your head, all the way down to the tips of your toes.

Now place your hand on your heart.
Feel the comforting energy of the beat of
your heart as it moves through you.

Notice your breathing, as you feel the air flow
in and out of your nose or mouth.
Then feel your belly go up and down as you breathe in and out.

This energy that keeps you breathing, this energy that
makes your heart beat; it is your constant companion.

When you tune into it,
you can let it fill you with love and light.

This is the love and light that you can give
to yourself and to others.

It is a part of you, always present.

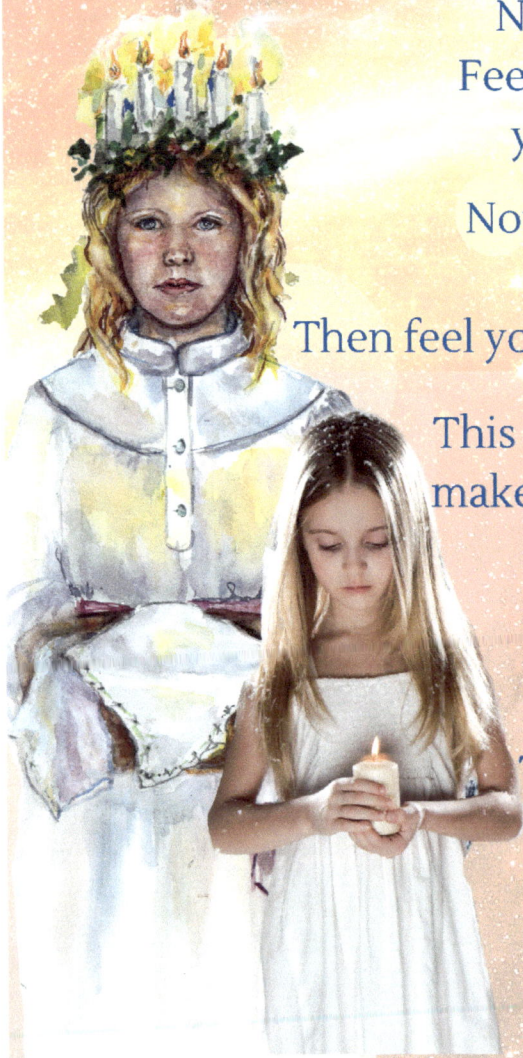

And now, take a few more moments to experience your
special place; the warmth of the sun, your heartbeat,
your breathing or whatever thoughts and feelings
come to you in this quiet space.

As we close this meditation,
I invite you to take in a deep breath,
and slowly open your eyes.
Feel yourself coming into this present moment;
awake, refreshed and at peace.

Welcome back! It is good to remember
that you can reconnect with this practice
any time you choose. .

"The mystery of God hugs you

in its all-encompassing arms."

~Saint Hildegard of Bingen

Thank you for joining me on this journey!

www.ingramcontent.com/pod-product-compliance
Lightning Source LLC
Chambersburg PA
CBHW042107090426

42811CB00018B/1871